SIGN LANGUAGE
FOR TEENS
Children's Reading & Writing Education Books

BOBO'S
LITTLE BRIANIAC BOOKS

educational & informative books for children
(PRE-K / K-12)

BASIC
SIGN LANGUAGE

BASIC WORDS IN SIGN LANGUAGE

YES

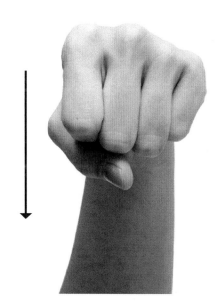

NO

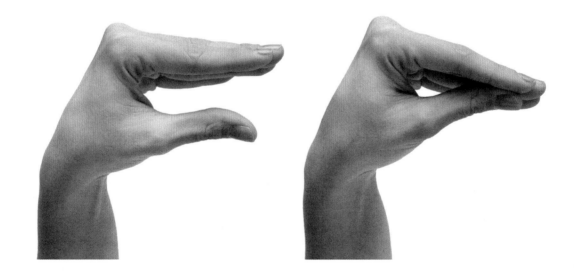

OK

HELP

TIME

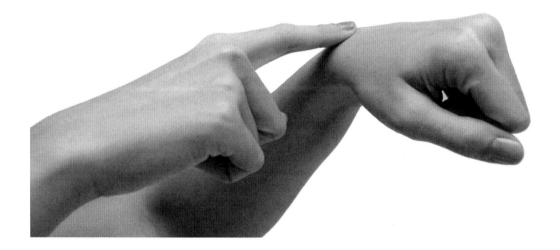

FRIEND

SAME

STOP

ALPHABET IN SIGN LANGUAGE

Aa

ALPHA

Bb

BRAVO

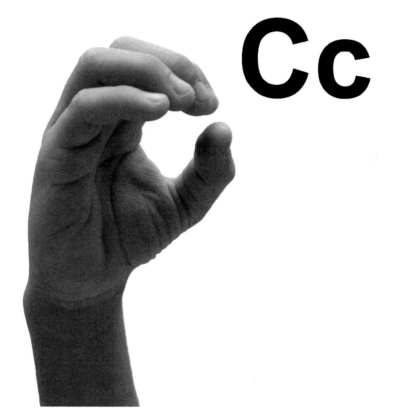

Cc

CHARLIE

Dd

DELTA

Ee

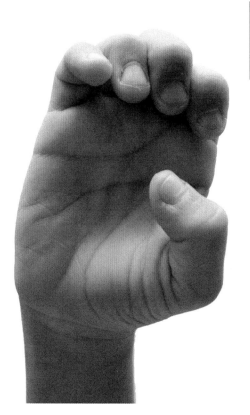

ECHO

Ff

FOXTROT

Gg

GOLF

Hh

HOTEL

Ii

INDIA

JULIETT

Kk

KILO

LI

LIMA

Mm

MIKE

Nn

NOVEMBER

Oo

ALPHA

Pp

PAPA

Qq

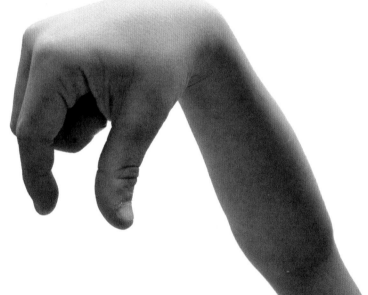

QUEBEC

Rr

ROMEO

Ss

SIERRA

Tt

TANGO

Uu

UNIFORM

Vv

VICTOR

Ww

WHISKEY

Xx

XRAY

Yy

YANKEE

Zz

ZULU

Made in the USA
Columbia, SC
27 November 2021